NEARING NARCOMA

By Matt Morris

Winner of the 2003 Main Street Rag Poetry Book Award

MAIN STREET RAG PUBLISHING COMPANY
CHARLOTTE, NC

ACKNOWLEDGMENTS

Some of these poems have appeared, in various forms, in the following: *Barbaric Yawp, Blue Collar Review, Cape Rock, 88: A Journal of Contemporary American Poetry, Free Lunch, G.W. Review, Manthology: Poems of the Male Experience, Midwest Poetry Review, New York Quarterly, Orange Willow Review, Poetry Motel, Poetry Now,* and *Red Booth Review.*

Library of Congress Control Number: 2003111709

ISBN 1-930907-27-3

Main Street Rag
4416 Shea Lane
Charlotte, NC 28227
www.MainStreetRag.com

To Dorothea

INTRODUCTION

Nearing Narcoma is hell-bent breathless more damned enjambing fun than a merry-go-round of monks stoked on love & death juice—hyped up on "Shempish" TV rural real and surreal sexual exhaust and exhaustion so thick you could backfloat on it—more vatic than Elvis's freezer full of Nutty Buddies Lorca's Mickey Mouse or "Frank/fucking Sinatra, baby"—hawking even more points of view than the P.O. missing person's corkboard Julio Cortazar or Medusa's hairpiece—basking in the physically metaphysical—imagine Dickinson morphed into Bukowski—twig to his sestina and free-verse acrobatics—watch out for this all too real language poet who knows how to work the raw material of the archaic to the ultra-contemporary—beware the technically innovative and very readable Morris Orphic finagler of lost love story teller and fabulist who pins the tail of the plot whether his own the world's or a swirling Dairy Queen of both on the particular—this is a poetry of bullets flying good humor double entendre uneasy moments real sadness and unvarnished beauty—Morris word artist running counter to our endearing cultural moment takes it all personally—paints and gouges the relief map of his American canvas ala mode de Van Gogh with thick palpable strokes.

Roger Weingarten

CONTENTS

I

II

III

IV

V

I

ASPECTS OF DAGWOOD

Dagwood dealing poker in Ed Feeley's garage; an unshaded
bulb blares over his pin-cushion head. At the table,
simple men puffing black stogies, quaffing frothy mugs.
The one with red hair, buck teeth takes the pot with three aces,
a king, & a queen, all the same suit. A fearful voice.
— Here comes Blondie mad as a goose, Dagwood.

Dagwood at the office snoozing at his desk, an unsigned
contract floating to the floor, pretty as a dream.
His comic cellblock switches from lemon to plum to tangerine,
serving to foster an atmosphere of insecurity,
fitfully punctuated by the business end of the boot.
— Dagwood! You do-nothing dimwit! You're fired! Get out!

Dagwood at Herb Woodley's hiding from the wife.
Dagwood at the pool hall making a three bank shot.
Dagwood at the bowling alley knocking down all the pins.
Dagwood at the doorstep bickering with a salesman's
onslaught of hard sell punches. Dagwood,
bruised & beaten, atwitter over his new gizmo.

Insomniac Dagwood with a fat sandwich of cold cuts.
Dagwood squawking in the tub when the ladies' club
drops by. Dagwood dangling from the bathroom window,
drippy wet towel draped around his bottom,
red Z's masking his face like a bland whodunit. Bells.
— Mr. Dithers wants you, Dagwood.

Dagwood whooshing out the door. Dagwood late for the bus.
Dagwood sporting the familiar bow tie & slouch hat.
Dagwood in polka-dot boxers, hiking his trousers,
pecking Blondie on the cheek, slurping down coffee
as he runs out, slamming pow! into the postman. Letters
flutter around them like fragments of Dagwood's recycled pulp.

THE SUMMER BEFORE LAST SUMMER

Taking the fishing trip I never had as a boy,
I'm standing on the boat's port side because,
well, I like standing, the handle of my rod
propped against my gut. I'm a man.
It's what men do. When I feel my line go taut,

I begin to reel it in. I'm not very good at this,
so it's a struggle. Nothing like Santiago's
great fish, I'll confess, but there's definitely
something on the other end. Maybe a hubcap,
maybe a fish. Like a pediatrician,

I have little patience, which
I expect to snap, that is, if my hands don't cramp.
I draw the line in, take up the slack
until, with just a gentle jerk, I'm left
holding a pole, limp & weightless.

My arms can't describe my loss. I stop, eyes fixed
on white fins cutting across the surface.
I think sharks, but upon closer inspection,
I see it's my old man, young again behind
the wheel of his '60 Plymouth, off on a binge,

driving home the long way, the wrong way.

DEGREES OF HELL AT HATTIESBURG

pour from a spigot like bad luck. You
drive naked outskirts hard for the freeway
out of a town whose one & only side's
as wrong as your last right. The dashboard light
blinks low fuel—to say nothing of your ego—
so you stop at a tumbledown station

for a fill-up. Map unfurled, you ask directions.
The towheaded attendant stares past you,
his thoughts drifting like fumes. I don't think I'd go
anywhere, he muses, & in a way,
you're grateful. Up ahead flutter the lights
of a very greasy spoon. You decide

on coffee & apple pie with directions on the side.
The oddly pretty waitress's mission
in life's simply to treat folks polite.
Yeah, right. I don't see it on the menu,
she cracks, painted nail scrolling for "free whey."
You plunk money on the table & go

blindly down a dead-end street. Years ago,
she might have fallen for you, tossing aside
pencil, pad & apron, running away
with your licentious imagination.
Now, obese & gray as a cloud, you
wait for the blankity-blank signal light

to turn gangrene. You feel a twinge of delight
cutting carelessly through the escargot
of traffic for a parking space, but you
leave the bar thirsty. You're driving. Besides,
they're closed for quote-unquote renovation.
Well, that's how they turn you away anyway.

You're too gullible. As for the thruway,
take a left at the dogleg after the last light.
A snickering cop gives you a citation
for something termed your failure. Your Yugo
runs hot through bleak countryside,
so you pull off. Your engine dies. You

wave for the moron yelling at you to go
around. Headlights flash. The blonde by his side
frames the gesticulation meant for you.

BEING & BEING DEAD

Perhaps the most
noticeable difference
is the lack of mobility. Not
only do overt motions
like lighting a cigarette
as you punch up work
or wife on your cell
phone to complain you're
running late, doing eighty
easy down the interstate
while rummaging
your stash for an apropos
CD or waving your hand
frantically at the screeching,
horn-blaring, diesel-
belching semi all at once
become impossible, but
also small,
internal movements — such
as those letting you discern
the tocsin of shattering
glass before doped-up,
burglarizing bunglers duct
tape your mouth & tie
you with anonymous blood-
stained nylons to your chair,
terrified — are done. In this
way particularly,
death distinguishes itself
from sleep. For instance,
the little girl, covers pulled
over her head, dreaming
she's a cloud while the red
house around her burns, never
wakes to the soot-smirched

face under the firefighter's
mask, who, lost
in a suicidal brown
study of smoke climbing
stairs that dramatically
drop into the paradoxes
of an Escher woodcut,
can't, coughing, reach her
or her deadhead daddy,
his mortal clump of ashes
smoldering in the embers
of his big ass recliner,
brew in one hand, righteous
doobie in the other, forever
nodding, watching
the eternal loop of *This
Is Your Life* reruns. You can't
be somewhat or temporarily
dead. Imagine your worst
nightmare, bug-eyed, flush
cheeked, smelly, mushy
flesh shrouded in a ratty, sadly
revealing mini when her
beastly heart suddenly revives,
wanting you to take her
to a movie & maybe
out clubbing later. Dead
is dead as an empty
barrel, minus the barrel
making its ringed impression
on your forehead, your
taunting, cursing ex's wacky
new flame fingering
your demise. You aren't
conscious of being dead, looking
back at the daffodils strewn
over your grave as you
ascend the celestial
escalator. For

having an awareness of being
dead is, ironically if not
gratefully, not dead,
but, you know, the other thing,
alive.

LOST STOOGES EPISODE

Geysers in the resident geezer's penthouse. Water sprays
everywhere, wrenches clank & clunk outlandishly
thick noggins, pliers clamp noses, yank
tongues & all at cataclysmic once, the flooded floor
gives way. With the boys
aboard, the tub cuts through stories
from a giant flip book: the curvaceous
blonde, fastening a garter, letting go
a tinny shriek, crosses herself in a modest X
as the tub wolf whistles past; the pint-
sized groom in long johns headlong leaps
a room below into the waiting arms
of his Alpine bride, who drops
him with a dumbstruck thud onto
the Murphy bed
          which catapults him

into the next world. A goldfish
in its glass globe double-takes, its spit-take
drenching the leather clad dominatrix
spanking red cheeked J. Edgar
Hoover, restrained by leash
from licking her spike-
heeled jackboot; startled, a trombonist, blowing
an extemporaneous "squawk,"
sends his brass slide crash-
ing through the window, slicing through rope
scaffolding. Doused with his own
whitewash, the painter dangles over
midtown traffic, frantically waving
at the prune who snaps shut
the obstinate blind that flaps
open to deliver a well-timed
whack to her self-righteous bustle.

But is this great hole in the edifice, this
apocryphal shaft, simply screwy

physics? one may wonder, staring up
starry-eyed & staggering, conked
kooky by the fallen tub. Or perhaps
a portal to heaven, out of which — in one-piece
striped bathing ensembles, snorkels, masks
& armed with plungers, sounding a litany of hellos
ascending the chromatic scale — come
the corporeal manifestations
of the gods, Moe the Magnificent, Curly
the Wise & Larry the Grand Vizier?
The hotel manager, a dead ringer
for long lost brother Shemp, the prodigal
Stooge who left the troupe to serve
the Ancient Mystic Order
of Pastrami on Rye, clamors
hysterically as a grande dame's double
strand necklace spills over the waxy marble
stairs upon which the bellhop somersaults
into the caterer, whose teetering
tiers of upside-
        down
             cake
                    smack
splat in the testy trigger-happy
house dick's face, whose snub
nose bullet snipes the goateed Austrian
doctor's cigar, clangs a serendipitous
gong, strips the toupee
from a monocled fop, kisses off
the shoeshine's two bit tip & lodges
in the Shempish manager's
heinie, who hopping around, fans
the papal smoke from the gaping
seat of his gray trousers, which
he extinguishes with a hiss
in the lobby's cherub studded fountain.
Jowl aquiver, he raises his gaze
to the abyss & prays, *Lord, if you're up there, help us —*
& even if you're not, help me.
                  Hallelujah. Amen.

WHITMAN SAMPLER

The last great poet has died,
having joined the immortals
for a softball game in the sky.
He lofts a deep fly to center,
his soul a can of corn.

That rummy Edgar Allan Poe
tags at third & foots the line,
testing the unknown arm of
aloof academician
Henry Wadsworth Longfellow.

I can watch them play all day
if I gaze into the sun
& stand on one leg just so.
And when the sun goes down,
I close my eyes & listen.

What slow summer evenings
I've heard the muse calling
Emily Dickinson — sliding,
cleats high, across the plate
in a cloud of dust — safe at home.

YOUR EYES ARE DIAMONDS

at a baseball game
in which a Texas
league single breaks up
the no-hitter in the ninth
on a two-out, O-
two pitch before
the paid attendance
of 43,000 whistling
maniacally when you kick
your stockinged leg
high as a Rockette &
your patented split
finger four seam round-
house knuckle curve
slider thumps into my old
catcher's mitt, the ump
squeals strike three
& I kiss you squarely
on the mound. Sweet
creamy nougat smothered
in rich milk chocolate, you
are my all-everything
center, anchoring
the line yet maintaining
your femininity while
I, the chiseled-chin
quarterback, smack your
ass & bark signals.
Standing tall in the pocket
I want to go long, but
Dick Butkus is coming
on a red dog, so I
eyeball the flanker's

quick slant over the soft
middle when boom!
You pancake the blitzing
Bear backer, letting me
uncork a tight spiral
to the wide-out streaking
up the sideline for six.
Flag on the play. You're
not the center, but the starting point
guard, a WAC sophomore
majoring in recreation &
an exceptional ball
handler. I'm your back
court complement, a slick
shooting small forward
with uncanny touch
behind the arc, a former
Diaper Dandy who never
lived up to the hype, but I'm
a senior now on fire
in the Big Dance, banging
clutch threes, man on top
of me, clock ticking
down when a true freshman
from Indiana beats me
off the dribble & takes it
to the hole untouched, but you
slip through a hard base line
pick & strip the buttery
Hoosier clean on the
double team & we fast
break the other way with
the acrobatic behind the
head between the legs jam.
Hooray! I'm the famous
Cap'n Spalding after big game
& you're the buxom blonde
safari guide, expeditiously
tromping aphrodisiacal

foliage, shooting a foam-
flanked, torch-eyed
elephant in your zebra
striped pajamas. Exactly
how an elephant got
in your pajamas, honey,
I wish I knew, but I'm not
really Groucho—I just
walk that way after kissing
your bumper lapping you
at Talladega, my wine
No. 69 Chevy spilling
into the retaining wall &
bursting into a barrel-rolling
ball of flame, my brief
career seemingly over. Yet
time in & out
we've skated cross-ice
through the crease, body
checked by slashing, high
sticking goons
on shorthanded
power plays, me at left
wing & you—yes, the center
after all, not only
on the ice, but in every
milieu, slapping the puck
like the Great One.

II

SHAM JEW

As if part of a shlocky
bar mitzvah shortly after I'd
turned thirteen, Mother told me
we had Jewish blood. I turned
to the ever suffering Jesus's
likeness nailed to our foyer wall.
Hallelujah! I didn't have to go
to Sunday school or so
I wished & blew
a month's allowance
on a 14k Star
of David & strung it
on a short chain around
my short neck. No longer
donning the stripes of my being
another Waspy kid from
the West End, I possessed
ethnicity! Oh I didn't
know the Torah & Talmud
from a tetrahedron, but
proselytizing Pentecostals left
me the hell alone, my shnozzle
buried in shmaltzy Yiddish
phrases as I shlepped along
the sprawling blight of blue
collar houses, frosted windows
filled with cheap flickering art-
ificial trees. When Grandma
arrived, fat arms swollen
with gifts, flushed joy
of the season rushed from her
cheeks the instant she glimpsed
my star pendant twinkling
in the flashing "Noel" strung
across the door. She called

it "jewry" & wondered aloud
if I'd outgrown my present, her
insinuation falling between
extortion & exorcism, but
no squelching pair of corduroys
insidiously hidden by fancy
foil wrapping could win me over
to that petty, three-headed
cloud-dwelling god I'd long ago
relegated to the realm
of science fiction. She feigned
surprise when I took my seat
at the dinner table & bowing her
head, pointedly asked
if I'd mind that she said grace.
You want to shmooze with your
imaginary friend, I began, her
anti-Semitic slips dangling
like tattered, yellowed lace
below the hem of her brown
polka dotted circus
tent of a dress, where suppressed
with sexuality under layers
upon layers of old ladies'
unmentionables lay
the saga of her mythopoetic
father, whose name no one
ever spoke, not even the one
he'd chosen to keep secret
that part he himself denied. Still
I knew how he'd died — parked
on the railroad tracks smooching
with his Jewish jezebel, too much
of a shnorrer to drive
to lover's leap when the train
came out of nowhere, whistle
howling. Grandma
swore her father's ghost appeared
confessing he was sorry for

all of it. For being
no good. For believing
everything was a lie. For being
a shlemiel, a shlimazl & a shmo.

TINY AIRPORTS

The fog lifts. You glimpse
the wires holding up
the plane, scuffed wing
tips of angels who guide it along

peeking out from a cardboard
cut-out cloud—that dark
fat one, for instance,
following you. What

did you expect—whirring
propellers of some gray
puddle-jumping albatross
to glide across the sun's

smiley button face? Up here
home is but a speck
on the glass, your career
even less significant—as if that's

possible. The drunk
next to you wants to hold
hands for luck, but surely he
sees through the guise

of your humanity.
Way down below,
the runway sticks out its sleek
black tongue to taste

a metal snowflake.

BREAKDOWN

A crescent wrenched
man lies on his back-
side on the gravel
shoulder under
a greasy fender, his crooked
legs poking out
from his jacked-up jalopy
wobbling in the draft
of passing traffic, his eyes
fixed upon the sludge
encased metal
mess of wires joining
doodads to whatnots
to disconnected
thoughts of his trunk
loaded with a lost
lifetime of luggage, his sun hot
seat lousy with crumpled paper
cups, dried-up promotional
pens, the heel-pocked map
for the soul that won't
neatly fold or fit
back into the glove
box, the meager cookie
crumbs of love. He wonders
what went wrong, knowing
that he's losing
time, wasting light. He under-
stands the danger, peering up at two
tons teetering on a steel
prong over his sprawled
vulnerability, but doesn't give
two shits if the car comes
down, doubts

in his doldrums he'd even
notice, though as usual he's well
wide of the mark. The blue
whale of his clunker chomps
him into diametrically
opposed directions—his spleen
ruptures, his rib cage splinters
under reality's crushing
irony while his numb
feet stick out of an alternate
universe, one in which
his waning, however unlikely, spirit
lifts, glimpsing the heavenly robed
bobble-head—a gift
never given to his
estranged daughter who lives
with his estranged
wife—nodding on the dash-
board, reminding him
of the distance
between here & the near
mirage of last exit's
gas & golden arches. *I do not
want what is not
chocolate,* saith the bouncy
angel whose manufactured
grin, come to think of it,
seems more of a smirk.

SOLICITOUSLY

after work, I stopped to see
if you wanted some
of the sum
of who I was in those
humdrum
days at the market. I'd freely consign
myself to a bottomless
vault, I pledged,
for the privilege of spreading
& straddling your
ample stocks
across your portfolio,
graphically
rendering your assets' full
potentiality. What federally
backed bonds could devise such
copious earnings, I ejaculated, poring
over your hot commodities, my tasseled burgundy loafer's
toe barely in the door. Fidgeting
with your
locks, you abruptly popped
the top
of your money box,
& bingo! We broke the bank,
knocking the books
off balance,
burying ourselves
under a feathered
nest of spreadsheets. Once spent,
I thought it

sound   to   tear

through the remainder
of the booty, &

was it ever!
My figurative cherry
red Duesy
convertible, restored
to near mint, rolled over
& up the crooked leg of your private
drive, & rising at the
Dow's opening, knowing where I was
& who
you were, I slunk away
into the ticker tape parade, endowed
with the mutual
funds
of our adultery.

DAILINESS

The city burns. Steering my leaky boat
through the smoky swamp, rubbing
the ash & ember of civilization out
of my eyes as the alarm razzes, I row
out of bed, right into my well-
worn rut of shit, shower & shave. Slowly
the fogged mirror reveals a phony
lonely me sliding down life's dull
disposable razor, scraping off
the stubble of another

disturbed dream. Then it's
turn on the tube — where some fish-
lipped gun nut's shooting off
his bass-like mouth's opinion
that temporarily coincides
with my own, considering
the cornucopia of arms reasonably
priced & readily available to shut
the dumb fuck up —
& coffee. I'm finishing the pot

around noon when the doorbell
interrupts. A woman
with blood red hair pulled
into a long tight braid offers me
a tract that asks,
Are you saved? From what? I start
to shoo her. Global
warming? Terrorism? Tooth decay? Nightmarish
interest rates? My terrible, impossible
true blue balls? But I don't
say anything. The small

scar above her lip tells
the story of another woman, another
lifetime ago, who wrapped
her car around a tree, drunk
& suicidal, I guess, because of me.
However, praise Jesus, it's not
my crazy ex standing
on the stoop, wanting to
talk to me about god
knows what, but a sad, weary lady
holding out her hand, asking me if I believe
there's enough love.

YOUR MOTHER

harped whenever you played
her cumbersome coffin of
a console that served its function — to fill
a space under the living room window.
The Who so loud, so fast,

she whined they'd wreak
havoc, picturing her poor dull
needle panting in vain to keep up

with the dizzying 33 1/3 rpms
of hard rocking vinyl. Goddam,
she bitched & shrilled, your soul
to hell, but kicking back, guitar rifts
wailing from scratchy speakers, you

discovered the patience of Job within
the vial smorgasbord of her bedroom
pharmacy kicking in, oblivious to

your black lab pup, its short chain
wrapped around & around the back
porch railing, strangled, while
your shriveled, shrunken, shrewish

mother hunched over her ironing
board, naked & nagging at the chewed
pencils stubs of your insides. You slammed
out the door, blue shingles raining

from that pillbox house, hate drowning
her yodeled refrain, her false
falsetto fading at the insufferable song's
finale. Years later, you felt something

like your mother's crazy needle,
racing winding hill roads. Your wheezing,
coughing wreck couldn't go
fast enough, fuck whatever

the speedometer said, to make it
home before your half drunk
half-uncle slapped
his arm around your shoulder

like a Led Zepplin record & broke it
to you about your mother.

BLACK CAT

You're given a piece, a revolver
         reproduced in infinitesimal
                  scale, its details
         painstakingly difficult
to discern as the rules, but you're
        game, a player, Frank
           fucking Sinatra, baby, chairman
            of the
                board, shaking
    the old bones & letting fate
         tumble helter-skelter
              out of your palm
       into a blurry montage
       of boxcars,
           snake eyes,
             sevens
& you know what, & before you know it, you're
         lachrymose & loaded, yelling
Yahtzee across the card
           table at your sorry-assed
       self, spouting
           minutia about tree
   lichens or the like to your floozy, boozy
      wife for a hard green wedge
            to complete the trivia
     wheel which is your life, scraping
  up enough colored pulp
            to drop a red hotel
   on Marvin Gardens just in time
to catch your Judas pal
           before it's his turn to turn
   on you, turn you in, pro-
         claiming confidently that poor, portly
     Prof. Plum did that rich
        bitch widow Mrs.

Peacock in the billiards parlor
                    & how, but the odds
of conviction seem iffy
                    as God: there's no
body, only

                    the tiny gun you were given
when the game began. It's your last
                    chance, & you're heading
straight to the hoosegow
            without
                    ever passing
                    Go.

III

HOUSE OF THE DEARLY DEPARTED

As a boy, I combed the rooms,
hoping to find you hiding
in a closet, ready
to leap at me the instant
I opened the door. Instead
the cascading slapstick
of nothing, not even your knockabout
cardigan dancing from its nail. I peeked
up the lifted skirt around your bed to find
dust dusted over with dust. Crouched
behind the couch, just the dog
scratching. Out of the maze
I slogged outside
to call for you, my voice
echoing down rows of shotgun
houses, when a beautiful

red horse clopped up
the porch steps, its shining mane
a magic fire. Having never
seen such a beast close up, alive,
I gasped. The horse
nodded & reared like a statue
awakened, just as a short, round man
in white roped its neck; his pale assistant
jabbed a gigantic
hypodermic into its hind leg.
I cried as they wrestled
the horse, nares flaring, into the cramped
back of their refurbished hearse,
"Animal Control" painted across
the black doors. I wanted to tell them
to stop, that it was my horse, but it wasn't
really. It was my heart.

BREEZY APARTMENTS

Free of cage, Ollie the parakeet
flits about, from headboard to armoire to neglected
rubber tree, before settling
on Corrine's foot, his minuscule eye,
round & black, compelling her
to recall last night. Shivering,
she involuntarily jerks, & off he flaps
out the window.
                              Cars wind
along 2nd St., radios abuzz
with static, pop rock
& gabby deejays' dumbass
wisecracks. Across the courtyard, the odor
of bacon wafts through the air
where Ollie soars from sill to sill
spying on the neighbors. The Smiths,
horsing around in 4C, shoo him
with incantatory obscenities,
so he shells their sheets, gloppy white shit
exploding across expensive blue
linens. Harry, the slob
in 2B, stands erect on his mattress
screwing an ornamental flame
bulb in the socket of the chandelier. Wrong way
Ollie flips & turns, bearing for 6A, where
the tenants have spread a crazy quilt
over their pane, so he can only divine
the cause of the intermittent
squeals piquing his curiosity.

Meanwhile, squatting on the john,
Corrine muses over the shiny motor
scooter that sputtered through the glass
of the corner diner's customary
persiflage. Straddling his banana seat,

the mopheaded clown had plucked
a stringed balloon off the ceiling &, taking
a toke of helium, made his high-pitched
howdy-do. What had she expected
to find under his silky shirt —
a true heart, not a tattoo
of a snake, tongue flickering, coiled
around a crudely rendered nude? But like
Brillo-y tendrils pasted to his chest,
it was all infectious grin & greasepaint
that, in retrospect, looked deranged,
her orgasm faked when he impetuously
showered her with confetti.

Corrine steps into her bath
as the water rises to a flutter
of blue wings. Ollie,
puffed up with himself, perches
on the faucet, warbling: *Listen, sweetie, can't you hear*
the cheesy love song playing on
the squeaky accordion
of a sagging mattress? For spring
is not only the season, it's also the verb,
as the duo next door surely knows
I would guess seeing them bounce —
if I may employ the baseball
vernacular — high in the air like a textbook
example of a Baltimore chop!
Tweet, tweet.
                    Corrine, drawing
the razor along her uplifted
leg, can't begin to understand
the nature of her parakeet's peeping,
or why he cocks his head from side to side,
mesmerized by the stroking
motion of her hand, from just above her
ankle to her thigh. "Too bad
you're not of my species,"
she confides, "for guys,

however prodigious, are seldom profound.
Or if I were like you, perhaps we'd fly,
skipping from humpback to lunch at Eros' feet among
the pigeons at Piccadilly Circus."

Ollie watches his mistress's hand, a starfish
cresting the wavy kelp of her crotch. She bucks
suddenly from the tub to see
about the hubbub outside her bathroom. Corrine,
dripping with irony, leans out the window while
Ollie, unwittingly knocked
off his soapy perch, founders
under the suds. Savoring
the refrain of her light
laughter, he struggles with his vision
of the slight curl of Corrine's
eyelashes rimed with grief when she'd
finally retrieve his soppy blue feathered
form, cup him tenderly in her palm,
her sobs crescendoing to a wail. Right now,
though, she's dressing for the turkey
summoning her with the nagging
beeping of a tinny horn.
"Coming!" she yells. The door thumps. Curtains
slap the wall.

ANYWHERE LIKE HOME

Other girls
    wear pastel sweaters, cable knit
        stitching down the front, with tiny gold
            scatter pins over their left
                breasts, flatter than your diet soda,
            & gold necklaces with five beads & retro
        navy circle skirts with argyle knee

socks & ugly saddle shoes. At the back
    of the bus, the school twirler
        twitters in her naughty twang, showing
            off her "little thing" to slack-jawed
                jocks, the vestige

        of her virginity teetering on her errant
    baton when the bus bounces
across railroad tracks that signify
    home's straight ahead, sort of. Just
        beyond rows of trees, rolling bottom lands stretch

            out to the river & the hills & the loneliness: Is that
        a question? The old bus great
      for chicken, McNeer gives it the gas
    & grins, squealing
around a sharp curve, swerving too
    late to avoid a ditch. Something

        or somebody flies out a window.
            In the tall tangled weeds, the perky
        majorette lies virtually
      unnoticed, her long, thick, satiny
    hair blending with afternoon
shadows. Normal days, anyway,

      this is your stop.

LOOSE FEATHERS

News of a murder swept the streets & stuck
to my shorts. Pockets jangling

with change, I danced a crazy jig
to be free. Nowhere to go, but

my feet moved inexplicably
toward your house, dusk's air

thick with the linens your mom
pressed in the kitchen, her steam iron

hissing. You didn't know what I wanted, only
no baloney. *Nothing*

better than that, your mom liked
to say, smoothing the fabric

with her wrinkled hand, so that's what we had,
nothing. In your backyard, the dead

or dying white-washed tree's
bark pulled off in clumps in our fists, & we flung

handfuls at the dark. What did we know
about anything? When your boozy uncle asked,

pinching our arms, we looked up,
pretending the dots of stars were nails

holding up the sky. It was just June,
I'd turned thirteen, you were my girl,

& there was nothing, nothing to do.

HEROIC RESPONSE

Wrestling with a half-assed crown of sonnets, once more I
let what passes through my noggin become deterred,
not by grackles jabbering in the willows,
but rather by buzz saws chirping through planking,
followed by hammers applying the whammy
& of course, the stream of profanity they incite

from the laborers at the construction site.
If only they'd remove the plank from my eye,
then could I judge this raucous army
who for one purpose has been hired —
that is, in between the mandatory gawking
at the ladies & cooing leering hellos —

to raise a row of homogeneous bungalows
across the way. Until now, an "oversight"
in the Twin Oaks' charter continued blocking
development on this stretch of woods, "an eye-
sore," according to the decision rendered
by the current charter president, a Mr. Tommy

Peters. "For a little money? Oh, dear me,
no," he protested the protesters. "I'll make kilos!"
(Peters, gentle reader, as you may have inferred,
blessed as you are with keen insight,
owns the parcel.) To the acts of Charles I —
tyrannical, traitorous, murderous king,

his imperial head severed, with one thwacking,
from the rest of his imperious anatomy —
do I compare such duplicity. Enraged, I
envision the racket outside as Mr. T. Peters' gallows
being erected upon the selfsame site
which, before this defecation, had inspired

my half-assed crown, which, like the land, now lies stripped & seared.
No more shall I behold wood pussies frolicking —
the chipmunks, the stinkhorns, & the occasional sight
of the doe on account of the bullshit economy
of Mr. T. P., whose cupidity allows
no remorse. "Aye,"

Cromwell declared, wholeheartedly
advancing autonomy,
though to my particular way of thinking it still follows,
"what unsightly vanity doth burn mine eye!"

ONE NIGHT

Maybe you're like me, driving
nowhere particular when
you pass a hitchhiker
who resembles you to the freckle.

Startled, you fishtail around a curve.
To one side's the stone face
of the hill that the road's cut from,
& to the other, down the steep

slope, mostly pine & fallen rock.
You pump your brakes hard
& turn opposite the skid,
only now, doing a donut,

you're heading straight
for your double. Remarkably,
there's just a soft thump upon impact.
You know you ought to stop,

but nobody's within miles,
so you keep going, still thinking about it,
asking yourself, like me,
what you're doing with your life.

THE GLASS PLANT

Five years old, I found out
      Papa worked at the glass plant.
      How wonderful, I imagined — his days
spent within the enchanted walls
      of a magic garden where
      translucent green shoots sprouted
crystallized red flowers
      like the one that sat
      on the old upright
nobody played. Somehow Papa
      didn't seem the type. He hated
      fairies because they only
did pansies. I suggested
      they help do his wizardry
      instead, but Papa just
stared at me with a squinty eye.
      He also didn't like sprites,
      which is why we never ate Chinese.
Still, Papa must have loved his job,
      for every night he went out
      to admire his handiwork. When Mama
mentioned this, she sounded angry.
      She meant he was either on a toot
      at the beer garden — a trick
done with bottles — or sleeping
      around with a horse.
      It would've scared me, but
not Papa. I just give her a little
      sugar, he once told me
      in a sneaky voice, his face
like Christmas, all lit up.

MOTHER'S APPOINTMENT

Widowed nearly thirty years, no
children of her own, my not
so great Aunt Birdie agreed to
watch me in a pinch. Slumped
in her flowery love
seat, red horn-
rimmed glasses strung
around her wattled neck
from a coiled elastic
cord, she snored through

endless soaps & quiz
shows, leaving me to play
with a weathered book
of matches & old Spooky, but
scared of that
antagonistic gray fur
ball curled on her sagging
lap — licking, scratching, pointy
ears twitching, giving me
the once over — I snuck

upstairs to squeeze
under her four poster,
hollowing a place
between dust
encrusted boxes where I found
a wrinkled photo
of my dead uncle tied
to yellowed letters, vials
of dried ointments, a talon, strange
laminated feathers & a small
black spider which I squished

between my fingers. I refused
to come when she, awake
from her so-called
cat nap, shuffled
room to room, yoohooing
& yowling, waving the carrot
of a snack. When the steep
steps creaked, I swallowed,
held my breath, cheeks
puffed at the sight of her worn-out
pink house slippers at the foot

of the bed. I might
have remained buried &
forgotten forever, but Spooky
slinked under the bed
skirt, devil eyes
peering through me & I squealed
& squirmed to life. A bony hand
suddenly gripped my pants' cuffs, tugging
while that scrawny cat,
fur raised on its arched back,
hissed & clawed the air.

CLOSE TO HOME

With one good headlight, his Chevy
pickup flies up a hairy strip of blacktop
splitting the stumps of sawed-off
hillocks, man-made buttes
where double-wides plopped
side by side like cans of human
beans butt up against a weedy family
cemetery, its craggy slabs the scowl
of a monstrous Tiki god, thoroughly
pissed at the displacement. Poor
dope, he smirks, cranking radio
up & window down — shitty rock
& shitty wind smacking his bare
cheeks like an old aftershave
commercial. His weary lids' sandbags
dangle from frazzled strands. Running
over ghosts of rails at about sixty
shakes his truck so hard his eyes pop
wide & the glove box spits out
of its steel slack jaw the ratty manual's
browning pages, moldy portions
of his last Danish & his secret stash
of *The Truth They Don't Want You to Know*
8-tracks, which, leaning over, he's scooping
up amid erratic peeps at the road
when he catches sight of her — a gauzy
gown stranded on the narrow
sloping shoulder, the black flames
of her hair nearly indistinguishable
from the night's chintzy
backdrop — thumbing. He hits
the brakes. Hard. Like every-
body, he wants something casual
as Levi's, only cheaper. Where you going?
he drawls, leering with x-ray vision as

she climbs into his cab's fuzzy red interior.
Wherever, she mutters over sudden
squealing rubber & like the cockeyed
quarter moon in the wavy treetops
grins strangely familiar. Remember?
her gray eyes seem to ask & instantly
she lights a cigarette, exhaling a blue
cloud in his red face. The weathered
matchbook from Roxy's like a segue
to a flashback slips slow-mo
from her bony finger's
pointy white nail. A distant neon
flickers in his head. No nosy desk clerk
requiring pseudonyms. No bumbling house
dick, ear to the door. No nympho-
maniacal maid to make a *menage*.
No vacancy, to put it simply, so he sticks
to memory's twisting two lane, trailing
a big rig's tail lights through pea soup, rubbing
his stubbled chin, still trying to place her.
She blows another portentous puff
in his glazed mug. Ah, funny how
the big book finally plunks open
to the crucial page. Flip that slick
son of a bitch upside down, right
side up, & its dizzy hieroglyphics
almost make sense, the way they did
back in the dying disco days
of the last century. Hunger, desire.
None greater than that funky
fire-gutted dive where he picked her
up, carrying her off the ashen dance floor
in the colored bleat of lights, begging her
to love him, her heart failing to respond
to serious mouth-to-mouth or even
the subsequent CPR, yet—
she's come back! He flashes
his gold canines. His clammy
paw creeps ever up her thigh. Stop!

she recoils. I'm an unworldly, unnatural, un-
holy thing, you stupid bastard. He pulls off
into a grassy gulch. Maybe,
he murmurs between slobbering
rebutted kisses, you've forgotten what
it's like in the sticks: Lonely. Hardly
any fun. Nothing but crazy, bad
road for miles — & cows
& they're not exactly our
kind of people.

SPIRIT OF THE DEAD WATCHING

Scraping caked, peeling paint
        under the eaves, I'm just
shy of the ladder's top, my disfigured
        shadow stretched across the clapboards.
It's about eleven I guess
        by the sundial I've become.
Through a gap in the curtain,
        I catch a glimpse of whoever
she is, in bed, curled up in a sheet.
        Whatever she's dreaming, I'm
dreaming too. For one can dream
        propped against the sky
of being somebody —
        like Gauguin, for instance.

Ah, Tahiti! I offer
        the dim reflection in the pane.
A tropic breeze brushes lush fields
        of vanilla beans & sugarcane
aromatically rising to the blue
        bedroom where I hover. Lazily,
the sleeper kicks the thin linen off & rolls
        over, her repose
the quintessential
        expression of *the truth*
stripped of artifice. In a gust,
        I brace myself against the ladder.
White paint chips fall
        to tarp-covered shrubs,
waving as if I should follow.

PIE

Excuse me, but you can't—
I said, waving a fork of the almost
hallucinogenic pastry—
change the will of an iron-fisted despot
who deems himself
praiseworthy by virtue of threat
of his hit-or-miss
omnipotence—& I'm not talking Fidel

Castro. Stop it! You're crazy
to question God, Mother riposted,
daubing her wizened face, a daisy
print napkin clutched between arthritic fingers.
All day you screw off like a magnum of cheap
wine, blasting your music so loud
it shakes my souvenir Graceland
plates off the wall. You won't
be happy till you've broken
them, like my heart, into shards
on the floor I just mopped. Thirty-nine & unable
to hold a job, you think
you can tidy up
the universe. God demands sacrifice, even if

only symbolic, as in prayer. The only
way—I spouted chunks of her
burnt crust, lacquered with a bizarrely
rich & salty cheese—I'd call praying
sacrifice is if you have money riding
on the outcome. Look, there are
no gods hiding behind nimbus-
capped hills to pitch
lightening bolts at the wicked & woo
at the good. I'd rather pray to a swivel
rocker, decadent & overstuffed, for I don't
need to flip a coin to decide if it's

there or not, in front of the big screen, despite
the years of wear & tear, providing
comfort to my

　　　　unemployed ass. Mother,
tossing her napkin aside, rose
imperiously from the groaning board.
Hmpf! You're fat! she scoffed.
At least you have a roof overhead &
food! I muttered

　　　　under my breath, feverishly
consuming the whole of Mother's offering until
nothing remained save
guilt & glut. That night found me
on my knees at the porcelain altar, spitting
out the devil himself,
when I had a vision of a sequined, gold
chained, giant Elvis, his amplified
footfall echoing like thunder,
& I trembled as he approached—

　　　　*Yeah, I know you're wondering what
does this guy know? Just
some fat cat in a white jump suit. Ever hear
"In the Ghetto"? But I'm not here to yak about
gold records. I want to give you
this Rolex. Now anytime you get the blues, mister,
eyeball your wrist, grab yourself
an armload of Nutty Buddies from the freezer
& you'll believe, all right. The King & the Almighty
are betting you'll find your life's worth
a whole bunch—just like that
customized, personalized
Elvis Dorado purring out front.
She's all yours—
so why not drop the top &
take your sweet mama out
for a nice
long Sunday drive?*

IV

NEARING NARCOMA

Monday morning's countless cars
drone back to work in a grave
procession of low beams.
Across the highway, I open up
my Fat Boy, V-twin jangling
loose change, pushing 85,
90, a dollar.
                    It's cold,
& the wind of speed makes it colder,
but something about a Harley —
I feel amazingly free,
even with Mother's straggly pink
hair in curlers, her claws clutching me
so tightly I gotta whiz. No one's
at the picnic grounds,
so I climb a rickety table, let it
fly, a completely human act.
Embarrassed, Mother
traipses off
                    after a dragonfly.
Chemical plant smoke drifts
overhead like a storm front.
I rev the bike. "Time
to leave the bugs alone!"
I shout at the shrubs.   Full
throttle up the hill, I glimpse
reflected in the gleaming
chrome assemblage a Picasso
of Mother in her cockamamie
housecoat & fuzzy slippers
hotfooting it after me up
the twisted blacktop, flailing
her flabby arms & mouthing
what I can't understand
over my monster 1340 cc.

She'll be winded soon,
so I let her catch up, let her
collapse against me, tears
smutching my oily jacket.
I should comfort her, I guess,
but it's difficult to talk
on a cycle, & frankly,
there's only so much anyone can take.

PHILOSOPHY MADE SIMPLE

My bones popped when you ran into philosophy class,
       out of breath, tongue dangling
from your sneaker, interrupting the lecture
       on dialectics. Hegel, Schlegel!
I wanted to ski the slippery slope
               of unsafe sex with you!
     Later, at the existential fountain, you said
that you were seeing someone, & taking a sip,
       I said so was I, which caused water
to dribble down my chin.
           The paradox of days passed
       like newspapers lost in thorny shrubbery.
Deus sive natura. I wandered in a drizzle up Alfred
       North Whitehead Way. The street lamp,
a loathsome thug, spilt my shadow on your stoop
       with an invisible hand. I knocked.
According to Aristotle —
              rain tapped my shoulder—
   virtue & vice are both alike in our own power.
I tried the door; it opened. *To secure one's*
       own happiness is duty, thunder echoed Kant.
Whereby I entered the Land of Beulah & waited —
       & waited. Drifting off
         in the proverbial lifeboat,
swinging Hume's fork like an oar, I slipped
       swatting the old priest overboard & fell
off the sofa, felling the oak coat tree, but no one heard,
       so did it make a sound? Swathed
in the fuzzy, brown logic
       of a London Fog, my head swam.
             Esse est percipi—?
More than ironic, it was moronic.
       Nothing existed outside
of me, foundering, or at the very least,
           floundering in the abyss.

FEVER 101

Mrs. Carey's purple
lap poodle paws
the school bus
wheel. "Pookie's
a good driver," she
brags, hands behind
her head to show
she's not steering. The loose
tailpipe sparks
against blacktop
like a slowly

struck match. I wake
in a sweat. Whatever
the clinic doctor
prescribed, I
substitute vodka
for. I lift the glass,
the fog lifts
like a hand peeling
back the linen &
I spot my acetylene
lover, her sudden
wings of virgin
wool aflutter. I
squint, watching
her disappear
in the vaporizer's
mist. A leather sole

crunches candy
on concrete floor. Pacing
Prof. Fishbean grills me
on the intricacies of
the Solzhenitsyn

plot, wanting names,
details, critical
analysis. Questions
rain, but I refuse to
crack. A swizzle stick
makes a good thermometer.

ON THE BUS

Not Kenny, but his crazy cousin,
            a disgruntled sex gizmo
sales rep also named Kenny, paws his hounds-
            tooth sports coat, digging
through his bulging
            pockets for *gum* or *gun* & chooses
the latter, chewing on
            the difference a lousy letter
can make — for instance, that one
            his lover — make that his ex —
sent to tell him it was over
            as they say, whatever
it is & whoever
            they are, the bastards,
their supercilious asses
            stuck to sweaty
Naugahyde. The steely
            extension of his manhood
glinting like the sly
            smile of the quarter moon, he
rises slowly, turns & boom: a seminary
            drop out, strung out
on angel dust, eyes
            firing with capitalized
Morality, abruptly
            flops to the floor, his beatific
wings beating willy-nilly
            against the floor's tin
drum. Big haired
            Norma, the webbed
feet of whatever weird, wild
            do she's trapped under
her bus driver gray cap, checks
            her mirror, screeches, steering
her first day on the job

precariously ahead, tilting
at a hairpin curve, nearly
            rolling, as in her troubled
sleep, over a sudden precipice
            before your all-knowing, all-seeing
narrator stumbles forward
            in his double-breasted black
suit & charges her to watch
            the goddam road while he wrestles
with the gunman, but your usually detached
            speaker discovers, much
to his chagrin, his omniscience's limits, for
            he can't stop, but only slow
via flashback the projectiles
            puncturing the semi-private
cloud of brand-X perfume spewing forth
            indiscriminately from Amy, divorce
pending, caked makeup unable to mask
            her antsy angst, rage or age, stroking
the hardened crotch of the cocky
            raw cadet who licks her neck, nuzzles
the hollow between her droopy
            breasts & loops a khaki leg
over her fleshy thighs. He thrusts
            his short arm up her hiked
skirt while the cunning fingers
            of his other unzips
her shiny black leather
            purse, his dirty jagged nails
plunging deep inside her
            well-worn pouch, groping
her crumpled sawbuck when a bullet
            zings through his liver
& lodges in her spleen. Another
            whizzes into the occupied
lavatory where Millie, pink flowered
            panties bunched at her ankles, is
heading back to campus after a quick
            trip to an out-of-town clinic,

& pings out the back
        of the bus, leaving the hapless —
homicidal perhaps — hitchhiker
        dead in the dust, his glazed gaze
fixed on the enigmatic G D
        LESS USA A L YO CAN
EAT BU ET $999 roadside
        diner sign. Kenny's deranged
cousin Kenny keeps
        firing until his clip's
spent, until your narrator, sensing
        the shift from gun-wielding killer
to impotent wimp, delivers
        an all-powerful roundhouse to
the gut, followed by a wicked
        uppercut, knocking Kenny
unconscious. Horn blaring,
        Norma slumped over
the wheel, the bus pitches
        into a tunnel so godforsaken not
even your narrator, tugging
        the tip of his goatee, knows
where the hell we're going.

UNCLE

Scattered clouds drifted through the bed
of a beat-up pickup hauling broken
mirrors to the dump. Such was your uncle's living—
if you'd call him alive. I wouldn't. The hole
in his truck's manifold roared demonically
when he skidded up the gravel drive. How stiff
I grew on the porch steps while you soaped
your thighs on the other side of the iron
shower curtain in my head. How hard
I swallowed when your uncle, pie-
faced & drooling tobacco
juice out the side of his split lip, plumped
his five gallon can of catatonic
gray insanity down beside me, snorted, swiped
his face with his sleeve & disappeared
into the cluttered garage. I leaned
back on my elbows. Probably your loose
silky robe had come undone
as you unrolled a nylon up your leg,
lifted to heaven. When the screen door
thumped, I hoped it was you
stepping out in your slinky red slit
skirt, but turning, found your
uncle scratching his balls, rolling
a toothpick across his craggy
teeth & making loud
sucking noises. Over a tarp-covered
heap on the lawn I leaped
like a white-tailed deer, afraid
of anything that moved.

METROPHOBIA

Under the moon, a shoe box
of contraband tucked
under your arm, your echoed
steps crack spidery pavement,
ensnaring you in foggy flats
of a dour town propped
against a cheesy
mesh backdrop. A black
T-bird chirps around

the corner. You duck
into a pharmacy, flitting past
the aisle of rain
resistant, sun repellant, plastic
delphinium. The druggist,
high behind the counter,
winks & smiles. In his lithic, dilated
pupils, you see the nozzle

of the drive-by
shooter locked on you. Stalking
the racks of prophylactics, I
pounce, pinning you
to the dirty
linoleum, my beefy
bulk your only protection from the
.45 whizzing by. Your name —

doesn't matter or
I'm sure I'd remember it, not
the post-impressionistic outline of the dead
druggist, the spotty
blood from a shot errant
as my desire. Unruffled, you
tell me to get off.

I already have, I mutter
sheepishly, hands jammed
deep in my pants'
pockets fumbling for
the compulsory cigarette

after. You gather
the contents of your box spilling
like a confession signed
with a red, wet capital "O" your
lips make abruptly over mine.
Another shot ricochets
off the register. Even though
I ought to hold you
for the cops, I let you go. Thanks
for everything, you coo in a
convincingly throaty way, but I
sense there's something you won't
say still lurking
out there in the big
whatever.

GRANDMA EX MACHINA

Grandma's fixing a pot
of something rotten,
        & I'm sprawled on the rug, glued to Saturday
            cartoons. "Keep it down. Your dad's trying
to sleep," Mom snaps, glaring at me.
          I hope that he can, but there's no way
            I'm letting my bitchy, brain-dead
       sister switch to her fluffy
pouf show without a fight. Only a dog
            could hear her high-pitched shrieks.
      The sonic boom
of Dad awakened shakes the house.
Yanking the belt off his wrinkly, all-night,
        post-bender pants, he wants
           to know who's first. I bow,
      always the gentleman, to my
         sibling rival,

            & the tip of his belt licks the back
of my legs, my head caught in a headlock so tight I can't squirm
      loose. Stinking like an abattoir,
        Dad finally stops,
      without giving little sister as much as a stony glance. She—
who gloats on a floor pillow & watches *The Bugaloos*—
      looks up at me & makes a dopey face, so I slug her,
          not hard enough to turn on
    the crying channel, but she still
        howls. Mom punches
a button on the remote & launches
     into her histrionics; Dad
        guns the Dodge toward The Blue Moon morning
of pickled eggs & shots. In the silence that erupts
     like a brown cloud,
        Grandma hollers from the kitchen:
         "Who wants oats?"

LA VIDA PADUCAH

When I lost my mind,
no townsfolk with torches
scoured my skull's
labyrinth, tracking gray
matter's minuscule
residual, wind

whistling through stalactites
of memory
like a batty spelunker.
See, I'd just finished

my first book, *Willie Diddle:*
Amateur Gynecologist,

at the Quik Shop,
& slapping it
shut on a fly, returned it

to the rack.
My ratty jeans bulged
with quarters, which,
in those days, allowing

for inflation, equaled nearly
jack squat. Working late
shift for the Colonel

only added to my desire
to climb three flights
to my efficiency & splatter
my brain like raw chicken
liver all over the walls—
& on the tube, the same

old drivel. But did that

make me crazy? Down
                    to his last life, Pac-Man
                              lowered the brim

of his weathered leather

fedora, determined
              to save his yellow ass
          from the sudden blood
                    red specter. Sniffing back the tears,
                         the black checker crowned me
                    "lovesick," protracted ash
          dangling from her cigarette

                    as I poured my pocket onto the counter
to buy Banana Nut Flakes,
          turkey jerky & *Swank*.

Such emptiness —

          tsked Dr. La Flesche, shining
                    a flashlight in my ear &
          grunting at the shadow
puppets of my genitals

              dancing on the wall — comes
          from wanting too much. Now turn
                    your head & cough. True,
she wasn't a doctor *per se*,
          but she was, ahem,
                    a highly regarded professional.

V

BUNCH OF JUNK ABOUT CHROME

Remember when the world sparkled. How
the gods shone with polish in bygone days,
their glistening munificence shellacking
their golden, self-damned heavens, layers

of enamel glossing over the nimbus
haloing you. How light afoot you gamboled
through the iridescent drifts
of that kaleidoscopic fall. How brilliantly

you played the glockenspiel & winked
at the scherzando — & phooey! How
would you ever take a shine to me?
The "me" reflected everywhere,

from the Studebaker's buff chrome bumpers
to the once popular stovepipe hats,
back then fashioned from silver & tin.
Against the glint of history, you stand apart,

your face inside the coin jar ever
beaming, ever radiant to this day,
untarnished by the change waxing over you
in a glimmering, shimmering heap.

Not the former Mouseketeer with dubious singing aspirations, nor the St. Louis Cardinals' pitching ace who, in 2001, posted a 22-8 record with a 3.16 ERA and finished third in the Cy Young Award voting, Matt Morris received a Master of Arts degree from the University of Southern Mississippi's Center for Writers at Hattiesburg, where he married the mad daughter of an alcoholic wharfinger, despite the admonitions of friends, family, some weedy guy in a big flowered shirt he met at a party and other  well-wishers, but this remains a private matter which he chooses not to discuss. Now divorced, he teaches in West Virginia, where he lives with his teenage son in the yellow house on the left after the third light. Usually a cream Camaro sits in the drive.